Vampire Kisses

BLOOD RELATIUES

VOLUME I

Ellen Schreiber

Art by rem

HAMBURG // LONDON // LOS ANGELES // TOKYO

HarperCollins *Children's Books*

Vampire Kisses: Blood Relatives Vol. 1

VP of Production - Ron Klamert
Editor-in-Chief - Rob Tokar
Publisher - Mike Kiley
President and C.O.O. - John Parker
C.E.O. and Chief Creative Officer - Stuart Levy

A **TOKYOPOP** Manga

TOKYOPOP and 🐾 are trademarks or registered trademarks of TOKYOPOP Inc.

TOKYOPOP Inc.
5900 Wilshire Blvd., Suite 2000
Los Angeles, CA 90036

E-mail: info@TOKYOPOP.com
Come visit us online at www.TOKYOPOP.com

First published in the United States by HarperCollins *Publishers* 2007
First published in Great Britain by HarperCollins *Children's Books* 2007
HarperCollins *Children's Books* is a division of HarperCollins *Publishers* Ltd
77-85 Fulham Palace Road, Hammersmith, London W6 8JB

The HarperCollins *Children's Books* website address is
www.harpercollinschildrensbooks.co.uk

Text copyright © Ellen Schreiber 2007
Illustrations © TokyoPop Inc. and HarperCollins Publishers 2007

The author and illustrator assert the moral right to be identified as the author and
illustrator of this work

ISBN-13 978-0-00-726942-6
ISBN-10 0-00-726942-0

Printed and bound in England by
Clays Ltd, St Ives plc

CONTENTS

CHAPTER ONE
Vampire Picnic...................................... 7

CHAPTER TWO
Eerie Arrival.......................................33

CHAPTER THREE
Grave Matters......................................57

CHAPTER FOUR
Mortal Threats.................................... 81

BARK
BARK
BARK

Welcome to DULLSVILLE

MEET RAVEN MADISON: SPORTING BLACK LIPSTICK, BLACK NAIL POLISH, AND A SHARP WIT, RAVEN IS AN OUTSIDER AT CONSERVATIVE DULLSVILLE HIGH. CURIOUS AND FEARLESS, SHE'S NOT AFRAID TO TAKE ON ANYONE, FROM GOSSIPING GIRLS TO EVEN SCARIER, NEFARIOUS CREATURES OF THE NIGHT. AMAZINGLY, RAVEN'S GREATEST WISH HAS COME TRUE—SHE'S DATING A REAL VAMPIRE. THE ONLY PROBLEM IS THAT SHE HAS TO WAIT UNTIL SUNDOWN TO SEE HIM AND MUST KEEP HIS TRUE IDENTITY A SECRET.

MEET ALEXANDER STERLING: HANDSOME AND ELUSIVE, ALEXANDER IS THE TEEN VAMPIRE OF RAVEN'S DREAMS. HE LIVES IN A MANSION ON TOP OF BENSON HILL, AND ONLY EMERGES AT NIGHT. A SENSITIVE ARTIST, THIS PALE PRINCE OF DARKNESS HAS SOULFUL EYES AND A HEART TO MATCH. HE IS WITTY WITH A MACABRE SENSE OF HUMOR, BUT KIND AND GENTLE WHEN IT COMES TO RAVEN. WHEN RAVEN FINDS HERSELF IN TROUBLE, HE'S THE FIRST ONE TO SPRING TO HER DEFENSE.

MEET BECKY MILLER: RAVEN'S ONLY GIRLFRIEND, BECKY IS MORE SHY AND RESERVED THAN HER GOTHIC COUNTERPART. SINCE MEETING IN THE THIRD GRADE, RAVEN HAS BEEN BECKY'S BEST FRIEND AND BODYGUARD, PROTECTING HER FROM NAME CALLING AND PLAYGROUND CLASHES. BECKY OFTEN FINDS HERSELF EMBROILED IN RAVEN'S MISADVENTURES, BUT THESE DAYS SHE HAS SOME EXCITEMENT OF HER OWN. SHE'S HEAD OVER HEELS IN LOVE WITH MATT WELLS, A POPULAR BUT GOOD-HEARTED GUY AT SCHOOL WHOM SHE'S STARTED DATING.

CHAPTER 1: VAMPIRE PICNIC

You might be wondering why I'm wandering around a cemetery in the middle of the night.

It took me sixteen years to find the guy of my dreams, I guess I can hold out a few more minutes. Who would ever believe that my wildest wish, to date an actual vampire, would come true?

When my pale prince, Alexander Sterling, first hit our boring little burg, it caused a stir.

His creepy, gothic mansion on top of Benson Hill, built by his grandmother, fueled rumors that his entire family were creatures of the night that escaped from Romania.

Even I believed it after I met him and fell in love with his dark, soulful eyes, so dreamy yet sad. After all, the proof was there. He was never seen in daylight, he had covered mirrors in his basement, and he told me he wanted a relationship he could "really sink his teeth into."

But during our evening movie dates and romantic walks in the dark, he revealed himself to be a broodingly quiet and mysterious, but very human mate.

But just as I began a relationship with this sensitive, hot artist guy, I was in for the shock of my life. One night at the mansion we sealed our date with a heart-meltingly passionate kiss.

I glanced to catch a glimpse of his sweet smile in my compact mirror. There was no reflection. I checked it again, then a third time.

When he finally took me to his room to reveal his secrets, I hoped to find a coffin. Instead I discovered amazing artwork. Turns out in addition to his gothic charm, he was also a fabulous painter.

Then I checked my makeup.

No Alexander. He was really a vampire!

It was my darkest fantasy come true! Perhaps he didn't really sleep on an unmade mattress in his attic bedroom floor like a regular teen. Instead, he sought darker shelter during the day.

Yes, Alexander was indeed a real vampire, no fake fangs or faux blood. Ever since I was a little girl, I had dreamed of becoming one of the undead.

But now that I was faced with that reality, did I really want to bare my soul--and my neck--to my new love?

Was I ready to spend all of eternity as a cool ghoul?

WHERE IS HE?
MAYBE HE'S
NOT COMING
AFTER ALL.

A DARK AND
TWISTED PATH!

HOW
ROMANTIC!

FINALLY, MY PRINCE OF DARKNESS.

I'D KNOW THAT RING ANYWHERE.

I THINK I'M REALLY FALLING UNDER YOUR SPELL...

AH!

EVERY TIME SOMETHING CREEPY HAPPENS AND THE TWO OF US SEPARATE, IT'S NEVER EASY TO GET BACK TOGETHER.

LAST TIME HE LEFT DULLSVILLE FOR WEEKS AND I WAS SURE I'D LOST HIM FOREVER.

BRR...

GREAT. NOW I'M LOST IN A CEMETERY I'VE EXPLORED HUNDREDS OF TIMES.

WHETHER HE LIKES IT OR NOT, I'M GOING BACK. I DON'T KNOW WHAT ELSE TO DO.

I REMEMBER THE DAY HE WAS GIVEN THIS.

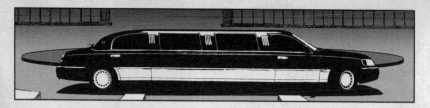

OUR EXTENDED FAMILY HAD COME TO AMERICA FROM ROMANIA TO VISIT MY GRANDMOTHER AT THE MANSION.

ONE DAY, SHE TOLD CLAUDE AND ME SHE'D LEFT US GIFTS IN THE DRAWING ROOM. WE WERE SO EXCITED.

I WANT THIS!

SHOVE

OW!

SO, I TOTALLY THINK HE'S GONNA ASK ME OUT.

WHAT'RE YOU GONNA SAY? HE'S KIND OF A CREEP.

I KNOW, BUT HAVE YOU SEEN HIS CAR? IT'S THIS TOTALLY AWESOME BEEMER CONVERTIBLE.

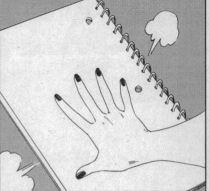

ENOUGH
DREAMING.
IT'S TIME FOR
ACTION.

ALEXANDER
NEEDS MY HELP
WHETHER HE
REALIZES IT OR
NOT. AND MAYBE
I DON'T NEED
TO GO NEAR THE
CEMETERY TO
START FIGURING
THIS OUT.

CHAPTER 3: GRAVE MATTERS

UNBELIEVABLE.

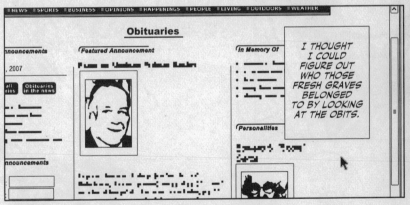

Obituaries

Featured Announcement

In Memory Of

Personalities

nouncements

, 2007

Obituaries
in the news

nnouncements

I THOUGHT I COULD FIGURE OUT WHO THOSE FRESH GRAVES BELONGED TO BY LOOKING AT THE OBITS.

BUT NO ONE HAS DIED IN THIS LAME TOWN IN WEEKS—NOT EVEN FROM BOREDOM.

SO WHO COULD INHABIT THOSE CASKETS?

I KNOW I TOLD ALEXANDER I WOULDN'T COME HERE AT NIGHT, BUT TECHNICALLY IT'S STILL AFTERNOON. I JUST WANT TO SEE IF I CAN FIGURE OUT WHAT'S GOING ON...

SCOOTCH

COULD THIS SUPERHOT CREATURE OF THE NIGHT BE ALEXANDER'S COUSIN?

WHAT'S HE DOING HERE IN DULLSVILLE AS PART OF THIS CREEPY QUARTET?

ANYBODY ELSE THIRSTY? I COULD GO FOR A DRINK.

ME TOO, I'M PARCHED.

CHAPTER 4: MORTAL THREATS

WHERE'S A CLOVE OF GARLIC WHEN YOU NEED IT?

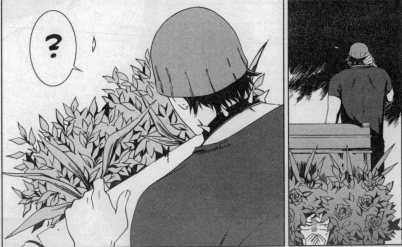

?

IT MUST BE SO HARD TO BE MORTAL. CAN'T SEE IN THE DARK. AND WITHOUT A VAMPIRE AROUND TO PROTECT YOU...

TAKES A MORTAL TO KNOW A MORTAL...

WHAT ARE YOU DOING HERE? I TOLD YOU TO WAIT FOR ME.

THMP

IT *IS* CLAUDE! HE'S HERE!

HE'S COME TO DULLSVILLE TO FIND BLOOD-FILLED VIALS YOUR GRAND-MOTHER HAS HIDDEN AWAY.

YOU SAW HIM?

DID HE HURT YOU?

WHY DOES HE NEED THE VIALS?

"sneak sneak..."

AS I WAS SAYING, WE HAVE SOME TRANSFER STUDENTS WHO WILL BE JOINING US THIS SEMESTER.

RAVEN, BECKY. NICE OF YOU TO JOIN US.

ALGEBRA 1

HA HA HA HA HA HA HA HA HA HA HA HA

GREAT. FINE.

NOW, TAKE YOUR SEATS, PLEASE.

THANKS, RAVEN, HOW ABOUT A TOUR RIGHT AFTER CLASS? I SWEAR, WE WON'T BITE.

HA HA HA HA

HA HA ...

WE JUST NEED SOME HELP GETTING OUR BEARINGS. SEEING AS HOW WE'RE NEW AND ALL.

YOU'VE OBVIOUSLY FOUND THE SCHOOL AND MADE YOUR- SELVES AT HOME IN THE CEMETERY.

WHAT MORE COULD YOU WANT?

DON'T BE CUTE, RAVEN. YOU KNOW WE NEED THE VIALS MY GRAND- MOTHER HAS HIDDEN.

YOU HEARD THE WHOLE THING.

COMING SOON...
VAMPIRE KISSES: BLOOD RELATIVES 2

As if dating a vampire wasn't hard enough, just when Raven Madison thinks she and her dreamy immortal beau, Alexander, will live happily ever after, evil rears its ugly fangs in Dullsville. When Alexander's cousin Claude and his crew continue to pose threats, will Raven do the unthinkable and betray Alexander? And what are the secrets behind the blood-filled vials that make them so coveted? With Claude and his gruesome gang willing to do anything to get the vials, it's going to take some quick thinking by Raven to thwart them. But will Raven's plan cost her what she most desires...?

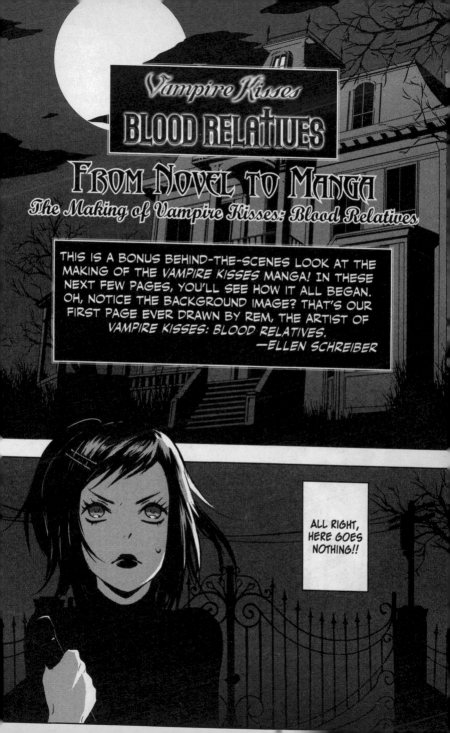

Vampire Kisses
BLOOD RELATIVES
From Novel to Manga
The Making of Vampire Kisses: Blood Relatives

THIS IS A BONUS BEHIND-THE-SCENES LOOK AT THE MAKING OF THE *VAMPIRE KISSES* MANGA! IN THESE NEXT FEW PAGES, YOU'LL SEE HOW IT ALL BEGAN. OH, NOTICE THE BACKGROUND IMAGE? THAT'S OUR FIRST PAGE EVER DRAWN BY REM, THE ARTIST OF *VAMPIRE KISSES: BLOOD RELATIVES.*
—ELLEN SCHREIBER

ALL RIGHT, HERE GOES NOTHING!!

RAVEN

HERE'S DULLSVILLE'S ONE-AND-ONLY GOTH GIRL GONE *MANGA-STYLE!*

ONE OF THE MOST DEFINING FEATURES ABOUT RAVEN HAS DEFINITELY GOT TO BE HER WARDROBE. BELOW, YOU SEE HER WEARING HER TRADEMARK BLACK BOOTS AND GOTHIC ACCESSORIES—LOOK AT ALL THOSE LITTLE DETAILS, LIKE THE SKULL BARRETTE AND BAT NECKLACE!

COMPARED TO THE FINAL VERSION OF RAVEN IN THE MANGA, THIS ONE SEEMS TALLER AND LANKIER. RAVEN'S FACE ALSO UNDERWENT SUBTLE CHANGES IN GOING FOR A SOFTER LOOK. BUT HER STYLE WAS SET FROM THE START. IT WAS THIS FIRST LOOK AT REM'S STYLE THAT CONVINCED ME SHE'D BE THE RIGHT ARTIST FOR THE STORY!

Raven's Fashion

When it comes to Raven, it's all about fashion, fashion, fashion! And with Rem's amazing sense of what's hot in the fashion world, she came up with a whole line of outfits for Raven. As the goth fashion-queen of Dullsville, Raven is always sure to look herself no matter what the occasion.

Just check out her P.E. clothes! It must be hot working out in all that black.

P.E.

at school

spiked hair

two tops

rings

Sheer black stockings

at school 2

wierd face

long fuzzy red black sweater

white, torn under shirt

straps from pants

no socks

at cemetary 2

under shirt & shirt same from school

skeleton print + white piping

long hooded top w/ strap sleeves

Sheer stockings pushed down

I love the skeleton jacket. I want one for myself! ^_^

Onion Creek

While most manga keep their characters in a single outfit, Raven breaks the norm in *Vampire Kisses*. Rem created all sorts of outfits so we could see Raven looking fabulous at every turn! Can you make out Rem's handwritten notes next to each item of clothing?

RAVEN'S EXPRESSIONS

WHAT WE SEE HERE IS AN EXPRESSION CHART. RAVEN IS DRAWN WITH DIFFERENT EXPRESSIONS, SO THE ARTIST CAN GET USED TO SHOWING ALL THE DIFFERENT SIDES OF THE CHARACTER. WHICH IS YOUR FAVORITE?

HERE'S MORE RAVEN...

ALEXANDER

IT WAS IMPORTANT FOR RAVEN'S DREAMY BOYFRIEND TO LOOK THE PART. WHO WOULDN'T BE PLEASED WITH THIS GORGEOUS RENDERING? IT'S EXACTLY WHAT I'D PICTURED. HE EVEN HAS THE SPIDER RING— AN EARLY GIFT FROM RAVEN—ON HIS LEFT HAND.

HAS THERE EVER BEEN A HOTTER TEEN VAMPIRE THAN ALEXANDER?

THANKS TO REM NAILING ALEXANDER'S APPEARANCE FROM THE GET-GO, THERE WAS NO NEED FOR MULTIPLE DESIGNS. OKAY, HE DOES HAVE MORE RIPS IN HIS CLOTHING IN THIS PICTURE THAN WHAT WE WENT FOR ULTIMATELY. THAT'S BECAUSE I ALWAYS IMAGINED THIS PRINCE OF DARKNESS TO BE AN IMPECCABLE DRESSER.

HERE'S ALEXANDER'S EXPRESSION CHART. I THINK THE IMAGE IN THE TOP RIGHT IS HIS REACTION TO ANOTHER ONE OF RAVEN'S DANGEROUS PLANS. *THERE SHE GOES AGAIN...*

BECKY

AS RAVEN'S BEST FRIEND SINCE CHILDHOOD, BECKY IS A VITAL PART OF RAVEN'S WORLD AND, THUS, NEEDED TO BE INCLUDED IN THE MANGA, OF COURSE. WHILE SHE DIDN'T GET A LOT OF FACE TIME IN VOLUME 1, YOU'LL BE SEEING MORE OF HER AS THE STORY CONTINUES.

REM CAPTURED BECKY'S CUTE AND SHY PERSONALITY IN THESE SKETCHES— THE PERFECT COUNTRY GIRL! I THOUGHT HER CLOTHES IN THE BOTTOM LEFT PICTURE WERE PROBABLY A BIT TOO OLD-FASHIONED, SO HER FINAL WARDROBE WAS UPDATED TO REFLECT HER LOVE OF SHOPPING AT, YOU GUESSED IT, DULLSVILLE'S MALL.

CLAUDE

AS THE MAIN ORIGINAL CHARACTER IN THE *VAMPIRE KISSES* MANGA, CLAUDE HAD TO BE SPOT-ON. HIS CHARACTER DESIGN IS SIMILAR TO ALEXANDER'S—SINCE THEY ARE RELATED—BUT WITH A BAD BOY TWIST. CLAUDE WENT THROUGH A LOT OF CHANGES BEFORE HIS STYLE WAS PERFECTED.

AS YOU CAN SEE ABOVE, CLAUDE ALSO SPORTED A VARIETY OF OUTFITS. WE BEGAN WITH A FUZZY COLLAR LOOK. THE FINAL DESIGN IS IN THE MIDDLE. HE'S MORE URBAN-PUNK-GOTH NOW—AND A TOTAL MENACE.

KAT

KAT WAS ANOTHER CHARACTER THAT UNDERWENT MANY DESIGNS IN THE EARLY STAGES. THE FIRST VERSION ON THE LEFT WAS A LITTLE TOO YOUNG LOOKING FOR A CHARACTER THAT SUPPOSEDLY DATED ALEXANDER IN THE PAST. IN THE FINAL VERSION ON THE RIGHT, WE SEE AN OLDER AND MORE MATURE KAT. SHE EVEN HAS TINY HORNS—AN ITEM THE ARTIST FOUND AT AN ANIME CONVENTION. I THINK IT FITS HER "DEVILISH" PERSONALITY.

ROCCO

AS THE MUSCLE OF CLAUDE'S GANG, ROCCO HAD TO LOOK TOUGH. BUT IN THE ORIGINAL VERSION, SEEN ON THE RIGHT SIDE, HE WAS TOO SCARY LOOKING. SO REM CREATED THREE VERSIONS OF ROCCO, EACH WITH DIFFERENT HAIRSTYLES. FINALLY, A KNIT CAP WAS THROWN INTO THE MIX. WHICH HAIRSTYLE DO YOU THINK HE'S HIDING UNDER THE CAP NOW?

TRIPP

HE'S SUPPOSED TO BE A TECHIE, SO HERE WE SEE HIM GROOVING TO MUSIC ON HIS HIGH-TECH PORTABLE PLAYER. JUST DON'T UNDERESTIMATE WHAT TROUBLE TRIPP MIGHT BE CAPABLE OF.

TRIPP'S DESIGN ROCKED FROM THE BEGINNING!

tripp

HERE ARE THE DESIGNS OF ALEXANDER AND CLAUDE AS CHILDREN. THEY ARE SO ADORABLE! I CAN'T WAIT TO SEE WHERE REM'S CREATIONS TAKE US IN VOLUME 2! STAY TUNED...

I awoke from a deadly slumber entombed in Alexander's coffin.

Since arriving at the Mansion shortly before Sunday morning's sunrise, I'd been lying next to my vampire boyfriend, Alexander Sterling, as he slept the weekend sunlit hours away, hidden in the closet of his attic room.

This was a dream come true. My first real taste—or in this case, bite—of the vampire lifestyle.

We nestled in my true love's bed—a claustrophobic black wooden casket. I was as blind as any bat; we could have been buried in the deepest recesses of a long-forgotten cemetery. Encased in our compacted quarters, I could easily touch the closed lid above me and brush my elbow against the side wall. The sweet scents of pine and cedar floated around me like incense. I couldn't see anything, not even my own black-fingernailed hand. No sounds were audible from outside the coffin. Not a siren, a bird, or the howling wind. I even lost track of time. I felt like we were the only two people in the world—that nothing existed outside these confining coffin walls.

Blanketed by darkness and a soft-as-a-spider's-web goose-feathered duvet, I was enveloped in Alexander's arctic white arms, my head gently resting against his chest. I felt his warm breath against my cheek. I imagined his deadly pale lids covering his chocolate brown eyes. I playfully fingered his velvet lips and brushed my fingertips over his perfect teeth until I felt one as sharp as a knife.

I tasted my finger for blood. Unfortunately, there was none.

I was so close to being part of Alexander's world—forever.

Or was I?

Though it was Sunday and I was exhausted from having spent the past few weeks protecting my nemesis, Trevor Mitchell, from the fangs of twin vampires, Jagger and Luna Maxwell, I was restless. I couldn't change my sleeping pattern from night to day.

Cuddling close to Alexander and sharing his world, I wanted nothing more than to spend our time kissing, playing, and talking.

But as he slept tranquilly, I could only think of one thing: A preteen vampire had descended upon Dullsville. And his name was Valentine.

The younger brother of the nefarious Nosferatu twins had arisen from his own petite coffin a few days before from somewhere in the vampire world and had been spotted in Dullsville by my brother and his nerd-mate, Henry.

I could only presume what Valentine looked like based on my brother's description: pale skin, pierced ears, black fingernails. I imagined a smaller version of Jagger—cryptic, gaunt, ghastly. How cruel it was that Jagger's sibling was just like him, and mine the polar opposite of me. If only I had been blessed with a ghoulish little brother. We'd have spent our childhood chasing ghosts in Dullsville's cemetery, searching Oakley Woods for creepy spiders, and playing hide-and-shriek in our basement. Instead, I grew up with a brother who'd prefer to dissect square roots alone rather than dissect gummi worms together.

I wondered why Valentine suddenly showed up in the conservative town of Dullsville, far away from his Romanian homeland. Now that Alexander and I were free from the older Maxwell siblings, I'd set forth on a new mission—finding out the eleven-year-old Valentine's whereabouts and motives and keeping him from Billy Boy before it was too late. But during the sunlight hours, my brother and Dullsville were in no danger, so my mind strayed back to the only vampire I felt secure with.

As Alexander and I lay in the dark, entombed and entwined, I stroked his silky black hair.

There was no place for me in the daylight without him. I had accepted the dangers Alexander had so warned me about, but I couldn't spend an eternity in the scorching sun minus my true love. Didn't Alexander know how easily I could adapt to his world, sleeping together in our cozy casket, flying together in the night sky, living in the dusty old Mansion? I wondered what type of vampire I'd be: A gentle dreamer like Alexander or a bloodthirsty menace like Jagger? Either way, since Jagger and Luna had departed from Dullsville, Alexander and I finally had a chance to share our mortal and immortal worlds. However, there could be an obstacle in my way, now that Valentine was in town.

Alexander stirred. He, too, couldn't sleep.

"You're awake," he whispered sweetly. "I'm sure it must be hard for you to adjust your sleep schedule."

I didn't want to admit that I couldn't be the perfect vampiress.

"I can't rest with you so close to me. I feel more alive than ever," I said.

My fingers felt around his smooth face and found his soft lips. I leaned in to kiss him, but my nose accidentally bumped into his.

"I'm sorry," I said with a giggle.

"One of the drawbacks of dating a mortal," he teased, a smile in his voice. "But it's worth it."

"What do you mean?"

Instead of answering, he lightly touched my cheek, sending tingles through my body.

Then he pressed his lips to mine and raced his fingers down my spine. I thought I was going to die. My hair flopped in my face, and he did something I couldn't fathom doing in the dark.

He gently brushed it away.

I gasped.

"How did you know my hair was hanging in my eyes?"

Alexander didn't answer.

"You can see!" I said blindly. "You can see me."

"I'm very lucky," he finally admitted. "You happen to be quite beautiful."

There were so many mysteries to Alexander, I wondered how many more would be revealed to me—and how I could unlock them.

I buried my head in his chest as he gently caressed my back.

"The sun has set," he said matter-of-factly.

"Already? How can you tell?" I asked. "You can see that, too?"

But he didn't answer.

I could hear Alexander lift the coffin lid. He grabbed my hand and I reluctantly rose, standing in total darkness.

Alexander scooped me up in his arms and carried me out of the casket like Dracula holding his mortal bride. He gently lowered me and I hung close to him, unaware of our exact location. The doorknob squeaked and the closet door creaked open. I squinted as my eyes tried to adjust to the beam of moonlight that pierced the room.

We pulled on our combat boots as I sat on his beat-up comfy chair and Alexander knelt on the uneven hardwood floor.

"So, will you teach me to fly?" I asked, half teasing.

"Valentine is not the kind of boy Billy should be hanging out with. We must get to your brother before Valentine does."

With that, Alexander locked the closet door, grabbed my hand, and, for now, closed the portal to the Underworld.

* * *

Now that darkness had fallen over Dullsville, it was imperative that Alexander and I find Billy Boy; but I was torn. Today had been my first time really experiencing life as a vampiress. I never actually thought I'd get to spend the daylight hours in a coffin with a vampire. I didn't want it to end. As we reached Alexander's attic-room door, I paused.

"We need to leave," he said.

"I know."

I imagined my life with Alexander, his easel in one corner, my dresser adorned with Hello Batty figures in another. At night we'd wander the cemetery, hand in hand. We'd watch *Halloween* on his big-screen TV and follow specters in the hallways of his horribly desolate creaky Mansion.

Alexander extended his hand. I reluctantly let him lead me away from my dream world. We walked through the candlelit Mansion, past the huge rooms with sky-high ceilings, the wind whispering through the corridor.

At the foot of the red-carpeted grand staircase we greeted Alexander's butler, Jameson, who looked especially creepy today in his vintage black suit. He must have been staying out with his new girlfriend, my former boss Ruby White. His eyes were extra buggy, but his ghost white face blushed red when he spoke.

"Good evening, Miss Raven," he said softly in his Romanian accent.

"Hello, Jameson."

"I'll have dinner for you in a few moments," the creepy man said.

"I appreciate it, Jameson, but we don't have time for

that now," Alexander commented, like Batman to his butler, Alfred.

I felt a pang of loneliness for Jameson—he would have to eat alone in the Mansion.

Jameson looked relieved, though, and as we gathered our jackets, I could hear him on the telephone. "Miss Ruby? I'm available for dinner earlier than I thought . . . Wonderful. Yes, I would be grateful if you could pick me up here. I love a woman in charge," he teased.

I felt like we were traveling cross-country as Alexander drove us in Jameson's Mercedes down the twisty, winding, desolate roads away from Benson Hill to the immaculately manicured streets of my suburban neighborhood.

Anxious to find Billy Boy, I raced up the front steps and fumbled with my collection of keys—a house key, one front and one back door, a file drawer key, a diary key, and a few that I couldn't recall what they unlocked. All were attached to several key chains—an Olivia Outcast figure, a Hello Batty stuffie, and a plastic *Donnie Darko* picture.

My hands shook as I tried to find the right one.

Alexander calmly placed his hand on mine, his black plastic spider ring catching the moonlight, and took the faux barbed-wire key ring from me.

He quickly picked out my house key and put it in the lock.

Within a moment, we were inside.

"Billy Boy?" I called from the bottom of the stairs.

There was no answer. Not even a "Go away."

I turned to Alexander. He looked worried.

I flew up the beige-carpeted stairs and headed toward Billy Boy's room. A haphazardly painted sign with red-and-black letters hung on his closed door. "NO GHOULS ALLOWED. THAT MEANS YOU, RAVEN!"

I snarled and threw open the door.

"We need to talk," I warned.

Everything—desk, computer, computer games, sports posters, unmade bed—was in place in my brother's bedroom. Except him.

I searched the bathroom and the neatly kept guest room, but no pesky sibling.

I bounced down the stairs to find the front door opening.

"Billy Boy?" I asked.

Instead, it was my mother, wearing a mauve Ralph Lauren sweater and gray pants, coming into the hallway.

"Well, hello, Alexander," she said, her eyes twinkling. "It's great to see you."

Alexander was always shy around my parents. "Hello, Mrs. Madison," Alexander replied, flipping his hair back nervously.

"I've told you, you can call me Sarah," she said with an almost schoolgirl giggle.

I rolled my black-eye-shadowed eyes. I wasn't sure if my mother was happy that someone in Dullsville, much less the world, would accept me or if it was Alexander's mesmerizing chocolate eyes that were making her giddy. Or maybe she was having vivid flashbacks from her hippie days.

There wasn't enough time or therapy to figure it out.

"I'm so glad you both are here," she said sweetly. "I

just called you at Alexander's—"

"Is Billy coming home soon?" I interrupted.

"No, that's why I thought it would be a great opportunity for us to have dinner together. Just the four of us."

I sighed. Finally, after all these years of nagging me about the way I dressed, my mother was treating me like a young adult. Unfortunately for me, I couldn't revel in my chance to be indoctrinated into the circle of parental acceptance. I had other things on my mind.

"I have to talk to Billy Boy."

"He's at Math Club," she said, grabbing a gray vest from the hall closet. "They rented out the library for the year-end party."

"I have to tell him something," I said.

"We have reservations at Francois' Bistro. Your father had to stop by the office and is meeting us there."

"Francois'?" Even though conservative Dullsville was as small as a golf hole, Francois' was on the opposite side of town, miles away from the library.

"How about the Cricket Club?" I recommended, suggesting a restaurant closer to Billy's location.

"You want to go to the Cricket Club?" she asked. "I didn't think you liked that restaurant."

"What's not to like? It's popular and fun," I said convincingly.

"That's exactly the reason I thought you detested it."

I bit my black lip.

"I'll call your father from the car. I think he has the restaurant on speed dial," she said as she grabbed her car keys and led us out the front door.